Fairfax
811 Postelle
Sonnets for Sarah's d
31111035728581

Y0-ELY-662

Sonnets For
Sarah's Daughters
and
Selected Poems

Sonnets For Sarah's Daughters
and
Selected Poems

by

Yvonne Postelle

Dragonfly Press
Oakland, California

Published by Dragonfly Press
7285 Snake Road
Oakland, California 94611, USA
(510) 339-6974
(800) 566-6370 Access 01

First Edition

Copyright © 1999 by Yvonne Postelle
All rights reserved

Composition by Scott Perry of
Archetype Typography, Berkeley, California

Printed in the United States of America

Acknowledgments

Special thanks to Jannie Dresser, poet, workshop leader,
teacher and friend. Many of these poems began as exercises
in her workshops in San Miguel de Allende, Mexico, and
at locations in California.
Thank you to pre-publication readers Lisanne Aguilar, Eileen
Downey, Martin Friedman and Jack Peary for their helpful
comments. Thank you Pat Voss for proof reading the final
manuscript. Thanks, too, to Paul Mico of Third Party
Publishing Company, Adam David Miller, Poet, Sarah
Teitschal and John Weiss for their wise and helpful
pre-publication advice.

Library of Congress Cataloging in Publication Data

Yvonne Postelle
Sonnets For Sarah's Daughters and Selected Poems
I. Title
ISBN 0-89914-066-1 (paper)
98-94899 CIP

For
Margaret Estelle
Ida Elsie
Minnie Ellen
Ruby Lillian
Bertie Lee

In easy times
and in adversity,
they're Sunday school
and university.

Contents

For Sarah's Daughters

Remembering Oklahoma

Family

Requited Love

Heart's Weather

For Sarah's Daughters

Throughout my life, Mother
and her four sisters have
epitomized family solidarity. This
book, and in particular, the poems in
this first section, are celebrations of the five
sisters who taught me, by their example,
that the mantle of family love is ample to
accommodate individual differences and
contradictory points of view.

AS ELDEST I WAS FIRST TO BREAK AWAY

(Margaret Estelle)

As eldest I was first to break away
from the patchwork that made up our daily life.
You sisters say I broke our father's heart
by marrying one he thought was wrong for me.
For years we spoke like strangers when we met;
it's hard to love a parent who is right.

I stuck with Richard through some rough and tough
until at fifty-five I learned to drive;
I've lived my life to suit myself since then.
As we don't have forever and a day,
let's talk about our good times and be glad
that time allows our meeting once again.

We'll take what life gives out and not complain —
though you would be the first to understand.

HAPPINESS CAME EASY IN THOSE DAYS

(Ida Elsie)

Happiness came easy in those days. Born
between the eldest and the young, I crept
unnoticed toward a patch of sun
to play with rocks and nut shells by the barn.

When, at fourteen, Arnold called, I ran
not away from sisters but toward life.
Life was hard work — make no mistake on that —
when was contentment harvested from ease?

Side by side we slaved, brought in the crops,
together searched until we found a home,
protected children underneath the tarp
of family till they grew and had their own.

I live alone but live contentedly.
Blessed in you sisters and my family.

GOD GAVE ME TALENTS
BUT SO LITTLE TIME

(Minnie Louise)

God gave me talents but so little time . . .
Subject to Him, I followed husband, tended home
and kept my peace with neighbors and the world.
I never questioned always making do
nor asked for more than Dewey could provide.

We were as close as one in field and hearth,
with one voice cautioned children as they grew.
We never left the farm so I'm not rich.
And yet, I vow, I favor my small patch
as any rich man counting up his gold.

I raised my six, performed my duty clear,
and now there's time at last.
                                        Lap full of scraps
I sit and stitch my quilts the winter through.
They bloom like spring itself, like birds they sing.

I LIVED MY LIFE FULL TILT

(Ruby Lillian)

Though I've not had a drink these fifteen years
we all remember times when I was young.
My wildness started the night I saw
Richard kissing Margaret by the stove.
Though they were man and wife, my childish mind
thought he'd ruined her and kissing was a sin.
Well, I made up my mind to grow up just like Sis.

Out of four marriages I have got my son
two houses and the right to sit and rest.
You sisters tell me I should move around
should exercise my body and my mind.
I turn my back and turn the volume high.

Who needs to live forever, anyway?
I lived my life full tilt while I was young.

ARE YOU MY SISTERS

(Bertie Lee)

Are you my sisters, or are you Mama's ghosts?
You spoiled me as the youngest, now you chide
and say I leave too much in Harry's hands.
If Harry doesn't mind it, why should you?

And yet it's sweet to have you here this way,
five from a single womb and family all.
We eat, play cards, fill ourselves up with talk,
or shop around for clothes as souvenirs.

I watch you grow more beautiful with age,
made stronger by each hardship overcome.
Do blood lines bind us, or is love the glue
that's held us sisters well nigh ninety years?

Though life will give us nary an inch nor mile,
it cannot take the strength of five from one.

SUMMER IS STILL MY FAVORITE TIME

(Sarah Ellen)

Summer is still my favorite time of year —
warms my drying bones, brings those daughters near.
So brief their visits to my grave and yet
it's this grave keeps them coming back each time
to sit at table, tell the same old tales
of fishing, dances, school and first romance.

I held on, their rightful matriarch,
till cancer buried me at ninety-two,
and now its up to them to carry on.
Up to their young and to posterity.
I don't regret a minute of that life,
but it's not bad to be a memory.

And I won't be forgotten while my girls
return year after year as family.

I'M GONE SO LONG

(Walter Griffin)

I'm gone so long they see me as a dream,
a shadow papa who used to give them rides
upon his shoulders, on the coupling pole.
They bring me flowers, too, but it's her grave
they linger longer by, that brings their tears.
Men can't match women in how long they live.

As for their brothers buried here and there,
it's up to others to remember them.
I reckon that's why men pack up and leave,
go looking outside home to find their lives.
My girls don't purposely neglect us men,
they're good girls living life as women will.

Nor am I jealous of their Sarah love —
I know it's just the echoes of my own.

AS MAN AMONG THE SISTERS

(Harry Nelson Porter)

As man among the sisters it's my place
to see the larder's full, the tank is topped,
that they get driven where they want to go,
to stop for yard sales when they tell me so.
After sixty years they're so much like my own
I can almost tell you what they're going to say —

not that it's always been that way, and it's
what's not said that has the most effect.
I've seen hearts break, I've seen hearts mend again.
There are tales that I could tell, but never will,
that might surprise a stranger looking in.
But they all came back sisters in the end.

A house that's full of kinfolk's full of love;
I say a man can't have too many kin.

SONNET FOR FIVE SISTERS

(Yvonne)

As eldest daughter of the eldest girl,
I've watched and learned from you my whole life through.
Tenacious country morning glory vines
you clung to sisters and to family.
When lashed by drought, by hail and ice, by rain,
where others would give in, you said hold tight.

Five granite pebbles sloughed from the same cliff
and swept into life's unrelenting stream.
Through spring and summer floods you rolled and churned —
each on a path distinctively her own —
until more rounded, ever more yourselves,
you found your favored angles of repose.

In easy times as in adversity,
you're Sunday school and university.

Remembering
Oklahoma

OKLAHOMA PRE-SCHOOL

Before I learned to read I learned to work,
following in my parent's cotton rows
a canvas picking sack upon my back.
No one gave kids in fields a second thought.

My father weighed my sack, wrote down the pounds,
as day by day my tally mounted up.
By end of season I had picked enough
to buy a coat. They took me into town.

Rack upon rack in childish shades of wool
I looked upon my choices, took my pick:
pink piped in white, it had a matching hat.
Mama cut the tags; I put it on.

The power of money coursed within my bones;
still coursed there when the coat had been outgrown.

ROOSTERS CROW

*Roosters crow the day
awake, my childhood awake,
crow my past to present*

TRIUMPHANT ON MY FATHER'S BACK

Crickets chirred my triumph.
Frogs croaked in water's hidden places.
Fireflies, earth's stars, circled my bare feet,
lighted the dark hair of my father's wrists
where he steadied my exultant ankles

as high above my brothers
I rode upon his shoulders,
carried home through warm breath
of Oklahoma twilight.

Stars encircled my head,
swam into my ears,
sparkled in the blunt ends of my hair,
and crescent moon,
a curved and golden half-wreath,
hung from my right shoulder.

SPRING FERTILIZING

I feed my grass
as Granny fed her chickens.
Chick, chick; Chick, chick, chick,
she called,
broadcasting her grain
in half circles
from a cupped hand.

How many generations
have broadcast nurturing grain,
have sowed yes
against the world's
and nature's noes?

Chick, chick; Chick, chick, chick,
I sing.
      Grow green.
            Grow strong.

REMEMBERING OKLAHOMA

The house is gone.
No nail or hinge,
no flat foundation stone
commemorates desperate years
when we were born,
grew up and grieved
alone within that father-hewn,
father home.

And yet how green the grasses grow
in the meadow where the kitchen stood!

Above the reach of fox and feral cats
fisted post oaks offer shelter
to nests of small brown birds.
Patient parents, wings outspread, thrust
live red worms down ever-greedy throats
until one day, almost an afterthought,
they push the fledglings onto empty air.

Abandoned birds, like houses,
choose to fall, give themselves
to gravitation's thrall,
graze with outthrust breasts
the ripening grass

until panicked wings recall
the instinct for survival
and thrash indifferent air into a froth
that lifts the frightened creatures back
                              toward life.

THE GIFT

He gazed beyond
my shoulder at the wall.
His nervous hands
grew quiet on the quilt.

My statement hung between us
like the buzz of lazy flies.
They say I was your favorite
child, I'd said, hoping to recall
him to this room, this life.

Steps approached and passed the door.
Beyond the window pane
late summer insects
skated in the sun.

You were each
my favorite, he said at last,
a father's blessing
for six gray haired children,

and a lesson
in the tact and wisdom
that life requires
of all good parents.

BAREFOOT AT MY MOTHER'S HOUSE
(on the occasion of Mother's 88th Birthday, January 22, 1997)

Outside the winter orchard stands
awaiting leaf and flower and nut
and Mother sleeps behind her door
awaiting dawn, awaiting morning light.

When she sighs or whimpers in her sleep
I sit upright, ready to respond.
Barefoot, I cross the hallway to her door;
Her breathing quiets and I stop.

Silent I walk her floors
my only light the moon. No grit
or dust or stray hair pin disturbs
foot pleasure in mother's rooms.

As child I used to run, feet slapping
smooth worn planks of summer's floors,
and mother would lift me to her lap
while twilight held its place outside the door.

After last night's meal, it was I who swept
the kitchen clean, then sat at table,
eager for tea and cards and talk,
greedy to knit from words
garments for the heart.

Now she makes that grieving sound,
and I go swift, resolved to come between,
awaken her and interrupt the dream.
Again she's silent and again I stop.

Long I stand and listen to the dark,
the nearby keening of two wind tossed trees,
the plaint of bark on bark as they embrace
and bend and shield each other from the storm.

FRIED MUSH

This grilled polenta
which you called mush
comforts me as a mother's
breast comforts a tired child.

In this stylish restaurant
who will notice if I
put down my fork, press a finger
under the mushrooms and melted

cheese? I look to see
if anyone is looking,
then secretly suck polenta
from my thumb.

The taste and texture carry me
back to a wooden high chair where,
breast bone pressed against the tray,
I ate fried mush.

And earlier, Mother, on your lap,
sucking milk thinned mush from
your index finger, my first solid food.
My life is blessed:

this grilled polenta, your fried mush,
the certainty of mother love.
When I come see you Thursday
we will manicure your nails.

PUMPKIN PIE

As smooth and rich as autumn itself,
that amber sweetness pressed between
tongue and the roof of my mouth.

Sown in sandy hills, the pumpkin
furled wide its ropy vines,
collecting the last rays of summer's sun.

That sunlight coats my tongue.
In it I taste the earth, the air, the sky
the smoky smell of great-great grandmother's

Cherokee hands — oh, cinnamon and nutmeg,
allspice, brown sugar, high yellow yolks of egg —
grandmother love transforming vegetable to fruit.

UPON LOOKING INTO MY FATHER'S CASKET

Father, we shall not meet again.
The time for resolutions is at hand.
Shall I convey you to your grave
with love or hate? Now, before
the others come, I must decide.

But love or hate I'll place you
in memory's pocket —
a scrap of worker's chambray
worn thin as silk and faded
to the color of callused fingertips.

When I was still a child
and believed in hell,
unable to prevent the blows
that bruised my mother's flesh,
I wished you in that hell.

Yet, when mother left,
you looked so pitiful
I cried although my heart
was filled with pride
for her act set me free
to love her without shame.
Still I loved you, too, though grudgingly.

Husk of the flesh that gave me flesh,
it is easy to find the cause of hate;
what cause of love can I relate?

You peeled me oranges
When I was ill,
wrung water from a cloth
and wiped my face.

You told us stories
after supper's chores.
Warmed blankets by the stove
and wrapped me tight,
carried me to Granny's
feather bed.

Common memories
as unexceptional
as that tepid stream
from which we dipped
wash water for our clothes.

But now, the others come. . .
I will decide.

Father, the need to love
is greater than the need to hate.
Having grown beyond your strap,
the backside of your hand —
it's safe to love you,
so rest knowing that.

Let resolution not erase life's truths;
responsibility is a yoke, you said,
which once put on
cannot be cast aside;

so dressed in love and hate,
sleep quietly and unquietly,
the way you lived your life.

The way that I live mine.

Family

MARRIAGE HYMN

I slept beside you on the left that you
turning toward me in the night might stroke
with gentle fingers sleep-warmed back and thigh
until I woke enflamed with need and love.

Those were the best, the sweetest nights,
when, making love still half asleep, we knew
not who was moving in and out nor who
unfolded to the other like a hand.

In mindless love our bodies blended one
into the other, warm oil and water,
until passion satisfied and still entwined,
we slept the dream, connubial dissolve.

BEAUTIFUL DAUGHTER

You walk beside me telling me a story,
not noticing the heads discretely turned
as if to steal a drink from some deep spring.
I see them, though. Eyes that once lingered on
my hair my face when we strode side by side
now turn to you, and I've attained
invisibility. I've been eclipsed.
Were it any other I'd be jealous,
but I watch your ascent with quiet pride.
Beautiful as butterflies in flight,
with passion brought to every word you speak,
you draw admiring eyes unconsciously.

You help me cross the bridge from youth to age.
When all eyes went from me, they turned to you.

HOW SHALL A MOTHER

The sprinklings of gray hair seem accidents
as puzzling as the fact that he is tall
and moves about the world with confidence
and, when he's won new victories may not call.
His life is hard, and she's not there to help —
or, if she's present, sees him turn away
from words of mother comfort so she's left
to practice silence, play the stoic role.
How shall a mother love son grown to man,
how let go the memory of the child
who used to bring life's tragedies to her
for soothing explanations, comfort songs?

A mother must pretend her child's a man
until pretending grows and he is grown.

MONEY IS LOVE

Money is love, Kay Boyle said
on a rainy November morning
in San Francisco. Outside the window
the campus wore a misty quiet.

Her statement haunted me for a decade.
Sometimes I almost understood.
At other times I rationalized that she
had spoken metaphorically.

On this more recent November
I picked my way along Berkeley's
rain slick street and deposited
two checks into the mail.

When I returned home
joy exploded like a hand grenade
in the foyer of my apartment.
I have fed my children
for a whole month, I cried,
understanding
it was not a metaphor.

FOR MY CHILDREN'S FATHER

Everything I've got, I got myself.
Houses, carpets,
flowers in their pots,
tree framed view of bay with
mountains thirty miles away —
everything I've got, I got myself.

Except our children.

Anything I need I can supply.
Trinkets from around the world,
food from the fields nearby,
songs to soothe me,
poems to help me cry —
anything I need I can supply.

Except for children.

No grit or cleverness could wrest
that miracle of life not once but twice.
An ordinary miracle cynics say —
but I attest, and we both know it's true,
they are not ordinary, our two.

Thank you for the children.

DANIEL AT ELEVEN

Slender as a sapling and as tall,
he looks across my shoulder when he stands.
His hair's as black as ravens and his arms
can span the arc of eagle's lifting flight.

Concerning what to eat we're of one mind:
all food is good, but pizza is the best;
cookies and cream, dressed up in frozen curds,
deserves a reverent silence on our tongues.

We walk the trail to town and buy a book,
or play a game of Voyager and talk.
No need for explanations or for boasts —
We like each other just the way we are.

As night replaces day against the sky
the crickets' concert is our lullaby.
Life has not many pleasures more sublime
than grandson visiting
                         and summertime.

SLIVERS OF SOAP

Wet palms
coax perfumed lather
from their alligatored sides
and I wash my face
from the bones
of bath bars
others would discard.

Friends smile.
My family assigns
a motive
to my penchant
for using things up,
my penuries of youth,
but they miss the point.

When life has worn me thin
and brittle as this soap,
may someone need me still
until I break in the hand
or dissolve
in a fragrant act
of comfort
or delight.

I DIP MY BREAD IN WINE

For Sebastian Aguilar

I dip my bread in wine
as you taught me, Pop,
as your mother taught you.

A child in Estepona,
coming in from the fields
you pressed the red soaked

bread against your tongue
and waited for your mid-day
meal, her mother's blessing.

Later, in Hawaii,
you staved off hunger
with snacks of pineapple

and learned to love
dry dust between your toes.
Still, life is hard . . . even in Paradise.

And later painting railway cars
for Southern Pacific,
raising a family in a language not your own.

When cancer pressed its tongue
into your blood, you turned
away from food and memory.

Not even bread dipped in wine
could tempt you, and we
could find no words of comfort

in either language. Helpless
to ease your dying we could only
sit and share your silence.

Inarticulate then, inarticulate now
remembering you,
I dip my bread in wine

and tell my children and grandchild,
Dip your bread in wine
as Grandpa Sebastian used to do.

OLD HANDS

It is our hands
the young cannot abide.
Old faces smile,
speak the affectionate word,
sing grandmotherly ditties
to make a small child laugh.
Old faces are forgiven
lines and veins.

But old hands,
idle in an ample lap,
shallow skinned, veined,
time's spotted beasts,
these bring a shudder
to narrow shoulders,
an involuntary drawing back,
that fixed stare
of horror
and of dread.

I LOVE YOU, CHILD, BUT . . .

I love you, child, but run along;
don't interrupt me now.
A phrase half formed is on my tongue
a poem half born hides on that vine.

You're hungry now, I understand;
I'll feed you right away
but first let me write down this phrase
before it goes astray.

The book bags are all by the door;
Please grab yours and go on.
When you return from school today
we'll celebrate the poem.

POLONIUS E-MAILS HIS CHILDREN

Walk gently in the world and with yourself.
Think on those who've loved you, those you've loved.
Let your heart rest easy knowing
each is blessed forever by that love.

Look gently in the mirror of your soul
recognize the beauty that is there.
If you see bumps and pimples know that they
are seasonal eruptions not the whole.

You are not the pimple on your nose.
You are not the scrape upon your knee.
These brief distractions will soon pass.
Your goodness is the constant; hold to that.

Practice the gentle art of compromise;
When you can't have it all, take what you need.

NORMA'S GARDEN, SPRING 1998

The storm bruised all
the roses, tore the yellow
iris from its green,
battered the leaves
of peppers and snapped
tomato's brittle stem.

Only the west clump of peonies —
late blooming, who knows why? —
escaped unscathed.
Stern parent, restraining
voluptuous pink daughters
in hard green fists
so they alone survived
to signal spring.

WRESTLING GRANDMOTHER

December 1996

"Grandma,
wanna wrestle?"

Daniel is nine,
restless,
has cabin fever.
The snow has kept
us all inside
too long.

Four brothers
and I did not wrestle;
a country school yard
full of boys
and I did not
wrestle;
a husband
for eleven years
and I did not wrestle.

But this is Daniel.
Surprise my ambush,
I leap with arms outflung,
and pull his unresisting
body to the floor,
pin his wrists
the way I've seen it done.

Our laughter
rattles snowdrifts,
melts
the weather.

WALNUT HULLING

At walnut hulling time my family goes
to assist our relatives with harvesting.
Unskilled, unfocused, heads still full of town
we stand in running shoes and shirts from *Gap*
with gloves our only serious uniform.

We take the rhythm of machinery.
Just one question is at issue here:
throw out the nut or leave it on the belt?
Conditioned to exploring shades of gray
the answer's not so easy as it sounds.

Eyes and hands take over from the mind,
we lose ourselves in exorcising blight,
are startled when the huller stops for lunch,
and turn so sun can soothe our aching necks.

We wake to autumn's perfect afternoon.
"Look at this day," we say, "Won't you just look!"
as if cities were forbidden shades of blue
and genesis of joy were found in weather
rather than in sharing family's work.

Indeed, we hardly speed the harvesting,
and saying we are helping stretches truth;
suffering our help at harvest time
is a gift the farmer gives us out of love.

FOR DANIEL

Even a small cloud
placing itself against sun
casts a fine shadow.

Requited
Love

IF I SHOULD DIE

If I should die or you should die before me
the other would find others standing near
eager to soothe or salve the broken heart
to urge the widowed weep and hurry through
the time of mourning that numbs the eyes and tongue
to everything but loss. And in a year
or two or three, as these things go, someone
would tell a joke, a laugh would come.
                                        It's true.
Laughter will not die because I die
or even, my beloved, when you do.
Then appetite, though dampened, will return.
In time, another love may thaw the heart.

But oh how tepid must new ardor be.
I, loving without you; you, loving without me.

TAP-DANCING IN THE KITCHEN

I tap dance in my dream. The snow comes in
and floats in flurrying swirls into the pots
atop a crowded stove where I stir broth
and cook sweet onions in a buttery froth.
My feet have sprouted feathers at the heels;
I dance in circles, tending to my friends
and tending to a fragrant harvest feast.
Rich talks swirls up like snowfall in reverse.
Above the swirling flakes I glimpse the sky
brittle as ice and radiant with stars.
As I dance back and forth I smile and nod
and listen to your key turn in the lock.

IT IS NOT COURTEOUS

(For Jack)

It is not courteous to appear too pleased.
Though I possess the sun, the moon, the stars
and you, still I am told I ought to mouth
that liturgy of pain that keeps at bay
the notice of that who or which or what
might have the power to snatch it all away.

Besides, friends say, no one can be happy
all the time yet be in touch with life;
for life is mainly angst and niggling pain,
and aggravation's grinding day to day,
old age's maladies and loss of youth.
Well, I have you, and they have their advice.

Better to be thought prideful, simplistic and unwise,
than cloak the sin, ingratitude, in courtesy's disguise.

AS IVY, GROWING ON A FENCE

At bedtime, your hands
tuck the blankets around me.
I sleep soundly, secure,
palms open on the pillow
by my head

And wake to sunshine
at the window and a day's
slow progression toward
that intimacy which emulates
timelessness.

Gently as a feather which,
floating on a lifting breeze,
gains entrance to a locked
and walled garden, you entered
my life and settled on my heart.

As ivy, growing on a fence,
first takes support then afterwards
supports the fence, at some
indecipherable moment our separate
and simultaneous lives intertwined.

THE GARDENER

Each spring
I watch you
fall in love
with your garden.

I see your heart gladden
to each shrub as you direct
your seasonal symphony,
assigning each its place and part.

Under your ardent fingers
rhododendrons unfurl crimson silk,
petunias open yellow throats
to sing the drenched blue
sky of their petals .

Jasmine, heavy with love,
flings urgent tendrils.
Should you stand still,
it would entwine you,
lock you in embrace.

When you come inside,
turning to look back
at that suffusion of color,
like the jasmine,
I want to enclose you.

I brush a leaf from your hair,
lean my cheek
against the sun-warmed
back of your neck.

MISSING YOU AT SAN MIGUEL de ALLENDE

The fragrance of these flowers tortures me
but, Love, if you were only here
there is no other place I'd rather be

An orange bird lights in a purple tree
voluptuous in its plumage on the bier
The fragrance of these flowers tortures me

The sky spreads out like an inverted sea
Yet nothing in this town can be called queer
There is no other place I'd rather be

You did not steal my heart for it was free
I close my eyes and still you are not here
The fragrance of the flowers tortures me

The serpent breaks the pod and eats the pea
I stop at lunch and take a glass of beer
Is there some other place I'd rather be?

Though pain accompany love, I gladly pay the fee
When passion's past the flesh hangs dry and sere
The absence of your fragrance tortures me
There is no other place I'd rather be

INVISIBLE AGE

Anonymous as mountain fog at daybreak
or winter sunshine peeping through the space
between a curtain and the window frame,
I've reached an age invisible to strangers
whose gazes used to linger on my face.

Now I can stare my fill, and no one frowns
or turns to challenge me, to stare me down.
Only beggars and small children engage
transparent ploys, hoping to obtain stray coins
of recognition or regard. I walk
the streets with unaccustomed lightness
and live my life with unaccustomed grace.

I know that you'll be there when I get home;
it is your regard I count upon.

PHOTOS OF YOUR LATE WIFE

Photos of your late wife
smile from every room but two.
When I peel apples at the sink
her eyes watch every
movement of my knife.

Nor does your new house
dim her legacy. Clinging to clothes,
the dust upon the books,
she came a hide-away
to take residency
in every baseboard
cupboard, fireplace stone.

From the wall she gazes
unabashed at what transpires
within the living room.
Surely that fixed smile must turn
ironic when we cling together
on the floor, the couch, the hearth.

Across your back, she and I exchange
long appraising looks, a mutual regard,
and state the terms by which we co-exist.
Past love does not preclude
a present love; nor later love
erase love gone before.

ONE OF US MAY LOVE AGAIN

One of us may love again, not both.
May such new love be passionate and shared.
Now, while we may, let's make a pact that we —
the one remaining, the one re-loving —
will be generous to that new lover who
is blameless after all that he or she
has not my voice, your hands, our ardent lips.

If we believed in Gods we'd build them shrines
in thankfulness for present joys and ask
the gift of having each the other long
into old age and mutually expire
beneath a well worn comforter of love.

Ah, Darling, let us savor every hour
nor waste a moment guessing what may come.

WHEN I IMAGINE

When I imagine you as dead or love withdrawn
and me bereft of you as comfort zone
I do not think my life will ever flow
so smoothly or so tranquilly again.
Then I envision others on whose arms
I might dance a night or court with playful words.
Will others weave a web around my heart
and lace with lust my organs of desire?
                              I think not.
Though they be sincere and true as you
they cannot match your sweetness by a mile,
or should they be as sweet, they'd prove untrue.

I lock the thought of death away and turn
to greet your coming with a welcoming smile.

Heart's Weather

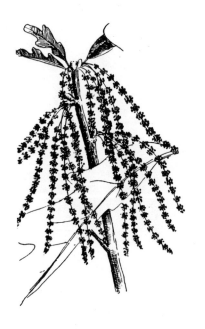

WHAT CHILLS MY ANKLES
COOLS MY SISTER'S BROW

A spider builds its web across my door
and wraps with lace the oak that gives me shade
to tempt the moth and catch unwary flies.

The bay fills up with summer's buoyant fog,
fog drifts northeast toward Napa and the farm;
what chills my ankles, cools my sister's brow.

Above the fog, the sky is eggshell blue
a gauze of small clouds intersects its curve.
Against the sky, in silhouette, my pine.

And west, between the fog and egg blue sky,
Mt. Tamalpais hums an ancient song
that says the world's both beautiful and wild.

This is my kingdom, my intimate domain:
Cocooned in spider's silk, in wool of fog.

HILL DWELLER'S LAMENT

That tree
obstructs my view
I want it down.
Yet so beautiful
in its green needles
does it stand

That I am forced to choose
as parents sometimes must
between twins born
with a common spine.

Like a banker
I take the measure
of the beauty of the tree,
the equal beauty of the bay.

Like a parent
I temporize.
I'll only maim
the tree,
let it survive.

THE DEER BENEATH MY WINDOW

Some nights as I ease toward dawn
and the day's lesser wakening
I hear whispered ivy torn from vines
and know the deer has returned
to share the night's reflected light.

The first time, unable to see the deer
because it stood so close beneath
my window, I crept barefoot
through that white light to spy —
only my nose and an eye exposed.

But it knew. It stopped its chewing,
raised its head. One must love
a creature that lives the night
as easily as day, that browses the wild
unkempt ivy beneath the light of the moon.

I had only to see it once.
Now when it comes I turn my face,
breathe the air it breathes
and fancy that it comes, in part,
to be near another sentient being.

But, if its goal is simply food,
may ropy vines of ivy grow
lush as spring grass all year through,
nourishing as autumn's ripening seed.

CREATIVE SLOTH

From dusk to dawn and dawn to dusk again
I spend the hours doing as I please.
I wake at four and write until its dawn.
or sleep till noon, then turn and sleep some more.

I read the weather from the clouds and sky
and contemplate the fog outside my door,
take tea and breakfast breads in bed, or take
them standing cool and barefoot on the floor.

Or rise at eight and hike a hilly trail
that wends along an eastern canyon wall,
then curves beneath a canopy of pines
where summer's sparrows pierce the ear with song.

Creative sloth is not for everyone,
but this profession fits me like a glove.

CRICKET'S WAKE

Last night I did not hear the cricket sing
until late late and then from far away,
and cricket's leg had lost its perfect pitch.
It paused in bafflement then tried again,
desperate singer striving to extend
the concert season for another year.

Each time the cricket sang I counted time
as mothers in recital halls will count
the measures that their children play on stage
as if to will that child and violin
shall persevere together to the end.
And while I counted, cricket labored on.

Till shade of sleep stepped toward me from the wall;
I woke to winter and the owl's call.

EMILY DICKINSON'S SNAKE

We met upon a warm mid August day
where each came solitary to the trail.
Both frightened: I stood rock still; it fled
a startled streak of terror, then it stopped.

Neither wanted the other's company.
Fearful yet courteous, reluctant to obtrude
upon another creature's solitude,
we waited, timid travelers, for a sign.

The light upon the trail, tilted and slant,
glowed like yellow glass held up to sun —
she had described this meeting perfectly —
with passport stamped and dated, I resumed.

How did the snake resolve its beating heart,
incorporate the terror and move on?

MATIN

When I refer to God I mean life force
or human love when it enlarges soul
or luck, or that sweet trick, coincidence,
or fate's propinquity to joy.

I meditate upon the smallest flower,
the two-leafed grasses thrust up by the rain,
spring and autumn locked illicitly
as winter turns away to clear its lungs.

Weaving doctrine out of nature's cues
I practice patience, let the patterns grow
and when I pray, I listen to discover
that which soul seeks beyond mere consciousness.

Wax, exfoliate, in Buddha's ear.
Dry salt of sweat upon the lip of Christ

STANDING A NICKEL ON EDGE

I fling a handful
of money on the bureau top.
Among the sprawl
of quarters, pennies, dimes
a nickel stands on edge.

That upright nickel
lifts my heart,
and I smile as I turn
out the light
and dream of standing
nickels on edge.

Next morning
the nickel rests
on its side.
Still, I separate it
from ordinary change
and all day long,
reaching into my pocket,
caress it with my thumb.

THE NATURE OF REALITY

After
months of studying
a mysterious
unblinking
red light
night after night
in a garden
across the
canyon

discover
it is the
steady
signal light
of your own
answering
machine

reflected
on
that window
through which
you
observe
the world
and time's
passing

THE WORLD IS EVER CHANGING

Awake to sun's reflection to the West —
rose colored, tender. Fleeting as love,
it fades as love can fade, but before I grieve,
a setting moon drops down to take my eye.

After the moon a crow tracks its own call
ponderously winging through the morning blue;
its body, sleek and slender in the Spring,
is stove black, solid as a fist, in Fall.

Beauty never fades without a gain,
a compensation to offset each loss.
The world is ever changing leaf to twig
spring to winter, morning sun to wing.

After the final change, what beauty then?
After the final night, what dawns may bloom?

SEASON'S CHANGE

I pause within a grove where birds at play
come close enough to fan me with their wings.
Nothing I know more quiet than their flight:
a silence, the air moves, they are gone.

Water trickles slowly from the spring
and makes its way along the canyon floor
while raptors circle lazily above
and insects hum late summer's monotone.

High in the tallest laurel, fall's first leaf
loosens, pauses, spirals ghostly down
and comes to rest with a prophetic sound
like the first large raindrop prefacing a storm.

A signal to the wind to slowly wake,
ready itself to rake the branches clean.

TURNING TOWARD THE SUN

Life fill me up
like that fish pond
cradled in the granite river bed.
I, too, would turn
my bosom to the sun
that schools of silvery fish
might swim from bone to bone
within the sun warmed
waters of my breast

GO AS CEASELESSLY AS THE SEA

Go as ceaselessly as the sea
with equally measured motion and
do not yearn for the safety of shore
once you are outside the harbor.

The sea moves from Hokkaido
to Mendocino and never once stops
to check the chart, to read the stars,
to gauge the distance left to travel.

AUTUMN'S PLUMS

I take them for ripe plums
then recognize
that's not the plum tree
holding fruit of brown.

Autumn's first dead leaves
curled tight like fruit
are ready to abandon
summer's home,

To slide the chute
of August
to the
ground.

SAN LEANDRO CREEK

For Lisanne and Daniel

Between steep banks
draped in purple
morning glories
the creek is full,
its current swift.
Beneath the bridge,
it serpentines and
makes a gentle murmur.

Just the kind of song
Pooh Bear might hum
when, drunk with honey
and affection, tired out
from a bear's adventures,
he drifts to sleep
in a patch of purple clover.

FOR THE MONTCLAIR HIKERS

I JOURNEY OUT

Each step is an effort. Each foot thrust forward
requires a conscious thought. Our bodies,
not unwilling, yet must choose to move.
Still, there are compensations going out:

freshness of morning, the unexpected breeze,
a cloudy hour to mediate the heat,
slither and rustle of secrets in tall grass,
and scent of fennel ripening in the sun.

There's exploration in the journey out
and fact of seeing things not seen before.
We fill our chests with air as from a pump,
inhale it, hold it, shape it as we walk.

We plod uphill, the sun upon our necks.
We reach the mark, and then the turning back.

FOR THE MONTCLAIR HIKERS

II JOURNEY BACK

Like a surveyor who has mapped the tract
and, light of heart, engages in small talk
we turn and face the trail head buoyantly,
knowing the hardest work has now been done.

The red of that madrone seems an old friend,
the eucalyptus tree has greener grown
against a sky that sings a paler song,
and poison oak, this morning green, is bronze.

Behind our backs while we toiled up the trail
each leaf and flower a little bit has turned,
the god of little changes was at work,
those changes lend a lightness to our steps.

So effortless our movements on return
our bodies and the trail ahead are one.

HIKING THE HIGH SIERRA

I

Too insecure to trust the elements
we pack and carry remedies for all
contingencies. Maybe starving refugees
would understand this need to carry home
strapped to the back while hiking through
thigh-high lupine meadows drenched so blue
our very eyes turn blue and we become
sky-eyed, dazzled, dots in nature's net.

Marmots, woodpeckers, butterflies and jays
move, luggageless, through variegated shade
and take for granted clean-boned granite cliffs,
the blue of alpine lakes glimpsed through green pines.

Blue flutter moth upon a blade of grass;
its silver outline pulses in the sun.

HIKING THE HIGH SIERRA

II

Because we're born with eyes, this place was made.
Each inch of granite, every casual leaf
holds beauty out like manna on the palm
of Christ to be devoured by reverent eyes.
Here nature sets examples for the soul,
teaches the moral life through metaphor.

Regard that pine. Bent double by the snow,
remembering the direction of the sun,
it twisted upright and began anew,
a dogged journey pointing toward the sky.

How straight the renewed growth beside the trail;
how true to its own nature grows the tree.

DEATH'S BRILLIANT EFFUSION

The fern's furled frond, traced with morning's
dew, glows roseate rust and pale translucent
yellow where winter's lolling tongue
has wrapped around it.

Thus begins death's beautiful effusion.
Engorged and flushed with all of nature's colors
the frond transcends in perfect brilliance,
then wilts and curls, transfigures into dust.

THE LAW OF REQUISITE VARIETY

Breathe deep,
seek clues in winter's mysteries,
juniper and damp earth
eucalyptus bark
dried and decaying leaves
beneath bare vines
yesterday's cut grass
and fennel — wild —
glimpsed through a wooden fence
with ruptured splines

Behind an ancient hedge
a farmhouse stands
encroached about
for fifty years by town
yet holding country patterns still
in sun-etched, shade-splashed apple lot,
in fig tree bare
as bleaching pelvic bones

And there, winter's strumpet also stands
resplendent in translucent globes
the season's ripe persimmons burn
above the aged alyssum's grainy snow,
glow in the honeyed smoke of time
that floats across lapped rooftops,
threaded power poles

And yellowed roses,
fragrance now transposed
by shriveling dews
and frost's tumescent tongue,
expire beneath a filtered failing sun
that falls more gently
than the gnarled hands of love

TAHITI TWILIGHT

Birds croaking like frogs
stitch earth to sky as they fly
enlarge the night world

MY NEIGHBOR'S GATE

(After Robert Frost)

Bereft of fence on either side
the iron gate offers a conditional welcome.
Beyond it, camellias burst with Spring;
my neighbor scissors their explosions
onto a yellow wicker basket.

I pause to ask if, children being gone,
the need for fences, too, is gone,
or if she leaves the gate unfenced
that deer may step more freely
into her garden's pink profusion.

Her back is an arc of concentration.
The gate divides us; I pass on.

AT THE FARM

Awake to hear coyote's distant bark
underneath, across and through the trees.
White tree trunks glimmer through a drifting mist
and orchard hunkers down as if to hide
in hopes that winter's blows will miss its chin,
that it can pass the season into spring
with some few leaves still clinging to its limbs.

Storm tossed trees, clutching those poor leaves,
as shriveled and yellowed as worn out gloves,
stand up and choose to wrestle with the wind,
trade howl for howl and, smiling, let wind win.
Turn loose your leaves and, naked, wait for sun.

When winter's full divestiture is seen,
then you may wear your amplitude of green.

TREES REPLY

(For Andy who said trees welcome winter's cold)

You are mistaken if you think we fear
the end of season, winter's cold, its storms;
we fear that summer's heat will last too long,
depriving us of hibernation rites.

We do not shelter leaves against the wind—
we do not cling to leaves; leaves cling to trees.
(In every family some are slow to leave
preferring what is known to what may come.)

What you misread as fear is fortitude
and resolution that has learned to trust
in nature's slow revolving, trust that time
will spin the wheel of seasons steadily.

It is not spring's green amplitude we seek;
when we hunker down it is to sleep.

AT THE SHORELINE
INTERPRETATIVE CENTER

I

How many
reconciliations we had
in the twilight of
summer evenings
like this one,

A month of felicity
and then abandonment,
body and soul each riven
in the parting.
You'd take both arms,
half the breast bone,
chunks of my heart, a lung . . .
You left the spleen.

When, in the summer solstice
of our lives, I welcomed you back,
it was to retrieve essential parts
as much as for the sweetness
of your eyes.

II

In this warm brown light
I sense you near
waiting for a word or smile, a sign.
We know I have the power
to bring you back.
And you the power
to go away again.

III

Time is as powerful as science
and callused flesh grew round
that old wound, heart.
A man-made lung,
magnesium pins to knit
the breast bone home.
Prosthetic arms that lift and carry joy.

Now flocks of seabirds
blur the twilight sky.
Beneath feather frothed air
I turn toward home
and cede you those,
now non-essential, parts:
arms, heart chunks, lung,
bone fragments from my breast.

Mount them on the wall
above your bed,
or store them in the soil
beside your door.

And plant thick bulbs
for April color
on that grave.

AN ARMY OF MOTHERS

Traveling west toward MacArthur Station,
through the train's window
I see block after weary block
of tightly placed houses,
their patched and scaling roofs
like peeling scalps glimpsed
through thinning hair.

As a duty I gaze upon them.
Hundred year old houses
needing care. This, too, is reality.

Then, in the sky clear blue morning
sanctity of home moves me,
and I see with certainty
that evenings discover
a holy universe behind
each faded and dusty door.

With elbow locked in elbow
these humble houses are
sanctuaries in platoon formation.
An army of mothers
clothed in aprons of grass
or geranium or gravel,

they stand silent watch
until evening
returns them their children,
adamant that no loved heart
sleep homeless or bereft
of family.

POETRY AND LIFE

I've lived my life till now as though convinced
life's more significant than poetry.
And that still seems the moral choice to me.
But now that art and life blend in one stream
I wonder at my courage to forgo
this art that's both my lover and my friend.

The better question looking back would be
how, children needing bread, could one choose art?

Contrary to youthful teachings, I now find
that choices made may sometimes be undone.
Children fed and grown, I choose again,
and this time choose that place of intertwine.

And I do not lament those years of life,
but wear them, diamonds, glittering at my ears.